Bob Frog has a bag with a tag.

"What is in the bag?" says Fran Frog.

"It is a surprise!" says Bob Frog.

Top Dog has a bag with a tag.

"What is in the bag?" says Fran Frog.

"It is a surprise!" says Top Dog.

Max Fox has a bag with a tag.

"What is in the bag?" says Fran Frog.

"It is a surprise!" says Max Fox.

"SURPRISE!"

Here is a 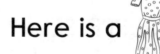 .

Here is a hat.

Here is an  !

"Happy Birthday, Fran Frog!"

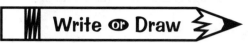

Write or Draw

What would you give Fran Frog
for her birthday?